Disney

Favorites for Two

Arrangements by Pete Deneff

Disney characters and artwork © Disney
Disney/Pixar elements © Disney/Pixar

*Based on the "Winnie the Pooh" works, by A.A. Milne and E.H. Shepard

ISBN 978-1-70515-357-4

Visit Hal Leonard Online at
www.halleonard.com

Contact Us:
Hal Leonard
7777 West Bluemound Road
Milwaukee, WI 53213
Email: info@halleonard.com

In Europe contact:
Hal Leonard Europe Limited
42 Wigmore Street
Marylebone, London, W1U 2RN
Email: info@halleonardeurope.com

In Australia contact:
Hal Leonard Australia Pty. Ltd.
4 Lentara Court
Cheltenham, Victoria, 3192 Australia
Email: info@halleonard.com.au

THE BALLAD OF THE LONESOME COWBOY

from TOY STORY 4

ALTO SAXES

Music and Lyrics by
RANDY NEWMAN

BE OUR GUEST
from BEAUTY AND THE BEAST

ALTO SAXES

Music by ALAN MENKEN
Lyrics by HOWARD ASHMAN

Moderately, in 2

BELLE
from BEAUTY AND THE BEAST

ALTO SAXES

Music by ALAN MENKEN
Lyrics by HOWARD ASHMAN

Spiritedly

CRUELLA DE VIL
from 101 DALMATIONS

ALTO SAXES

Words and Music by
MEL LEVEN

A DREAM IS A WISH YOUR HEART MAKES

from CINDERELLA

ALTO SAXES

Music by MACK DAVID
and AL HOFFMAN
Lyrics by JERRY LIVINGSTON

FOR THE FIRST TIME IN FOREVER

from FROZEN

ALTO SAXES

Music and Lyrics by KRISTEN ANDERSON-LOPEZ
and ROBERT LOPEZ

HOW DOES A MOMENT LAST FOREVER

from BEAUTY AND THE BEAST

ALTO SAXES

Music by ALAN MENKEN
Lyrics by TIM RICE

IN SUMMER
from FROZEN

ALTO SAXES

Music and Lyrics by KRISTEN ANDERSON-LOPEZ
and ROBERT LOPEZ

INTO THE UNKNOWN
from FROZEN 2

ALTO SAXES

Music and Lyrics by KRISTEN ANDERSON-LOPEZ
and ROBERT LOPEZ

JUST AROUND THE RIVERBEND
from POCAHONTAS

ALTO SAXES

Music by ALAN MENKEN
Lyrics by STEPHEN SCHWARTZ

With motion

LAVA
from LAVA

ALTO SAXES

Music and Lyrics by
JAMES FORD MURPHY

LEAD THE WAY
from RAYA AND THE LAST DRAGON

ALTO SAXES

Music and Lyrics by
JHENÉ AIKO

NEVER TOO LATE

from THE LION KING 2019

ALTO SAXES

Music by ELTON JOHN
Lyrics by TIM RICE

Moderately fast

THE PLACE WHERE LOST THINGS GO

from MARY POPPINS RETURNS

ALTO SAXES

Music by MARC SHAIMAN
Lyrics by SCOTT WITTMAN
and MARC SHAIMAN

Gently, not slow

REFLECTION
from MULAN

ALTO SAXES

Music by MATTHEW WILDER
Lyrics by DAVID ZIPPEL

REMEMBER ME
(Ernesto de la Cruz)
from COCO

ALTO SAXES

Music and Lyrics by KRISTEN ANDERSON-LOPEZ
and ROBERT LOPEZ

SPEECHLESS
from ALADDIN

ALTO SAXES

Music by ALAN MENKEN
Lyrics by BENJ PASEK
and JUSTIN PAUL

Moderately

THAT'S HOW YOU KNOW

from ENCHANTED

ALTO SAXES

Music by ALAN MENKEN
Lyrics by STEPHEN SCHWARTZ

TOUCH THE SKY
from BRAVE

ALTO SAXES

Music by ALEXANDER L. MANDEL
Lyrics by ALEXANDER L. MANDEL
and MARK ANDREWS

Quickly

TRY EVERYTHING

from ZOOTOPIA

ALTO SAXES

Words and Music by SIA FURLER,
TOR ERIK HERMANSEN and MIKKEL ERIKSEN

UNDER THE SEA

from THE LITTLE MERMAID

ALTO SAXES

Music by ALAN MENKEN
Lyrics by HOWARD ASHMAN

WINNIE THE POOH

from THE MANY ADVENTURES OF WINNIE THE POOH

ALTO SAXES

Words and Music by RICHARD M. SHERMAN
and ROBERT B. SHERMAN

YOU'VE GOT A FRIEND IN ME

from TOY STORY

ALTO SAXES

Music and Lyrics by
RANDY NEWMAN